A
MOTHER'S
Notebook

Design and illustrations by Cheryl A. Benner

Quotations reprinted with permission from: *Leo Rosten's Treasury of Jewish Quotations,* © 1977; *Fatherhood* by Bill Cosby, copyright © 1986 by William H. Cosby, Jr. (used by permission of Doubleday, a division of Bantam, Doubleday, Dell Publishing Group, Inc.); *Parents* Magazine; Phyllis Theroux, author of *Night Lights: Bedtime Stories for Parents in the Dark* (Viking-Penguin); Liz Rosenberg, author of a book of poems, *The Fire Music* (U. Pittsburgh Press) and of two children's books, *Adelaide and the Night Train,* and *Window Mirror Moon* (Harper and Row Junior Books); *Ourselves and Our Children: A Book For Parents* by the Boston Women's Health Book Collective, Copyright © 1978 by the Boston Women's Health Book Collective Inc., reprinted by permission of Random House, Inc.

What is overpowering is simply the fact that a baby is life. It is also a mess, but such an appealing one that we look past the mess to the jewel underneath.

Bill Cosby

My mother was the making of me. She was so true and so sure of me. I felt that I had someone to live for—someone I must not disappoint. The memory of my mother will always be a blessing to me.

Thomas Alva Edison

Having a family is like having a bowling alley installed in your brain.

Martin Mull

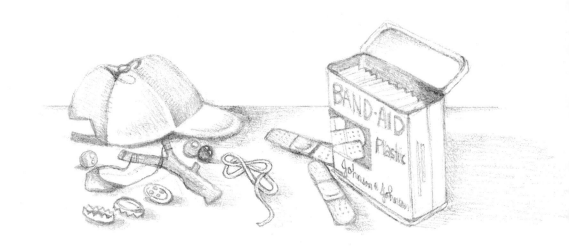

If you didn't have kids how would you ever know that teakettles shout or that the sky cries rain or that boats don't sink because they used to be fish.

We're the ultimate nuclear family, and sometimes I feel as if someone is trying to split the atom.

Georgia Houser

Your baby's first cry is the one you hear in the delivery room, the triumphant, tension-shattering sound that says, "I'm here, I'm breathing, I'm alive!"

Katherine Karlsrud

The real menace in dealing with a five-year-old is that in no time at all you begin to sound like a five-year-old.

Jean Kerr

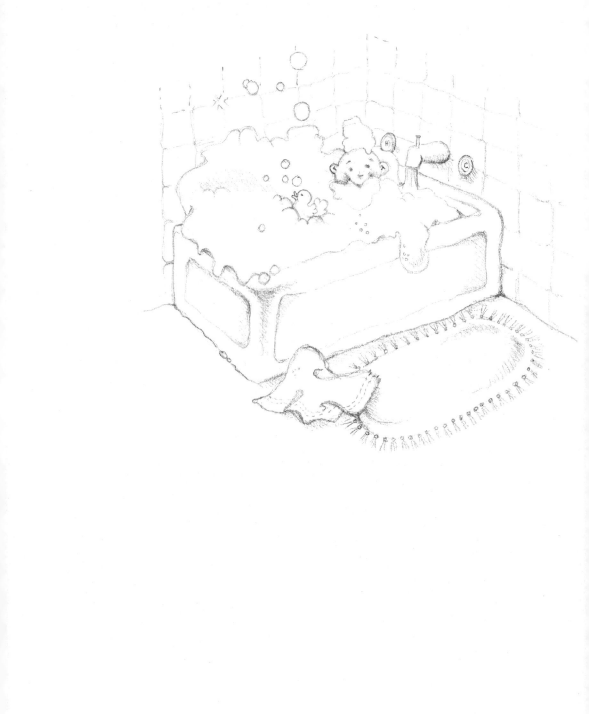

When we hear the baby laugh, it is the loveliest thing that can happen to us.

Sigmund Freud

Never lend your car to anyone to whom you have given birth.
Erma Bombeck

Mother is the name for God in the lips and hearts of little children.

William Makepeace Thackeray

Children are gleeful barbarians.
Joseph Morgenstern

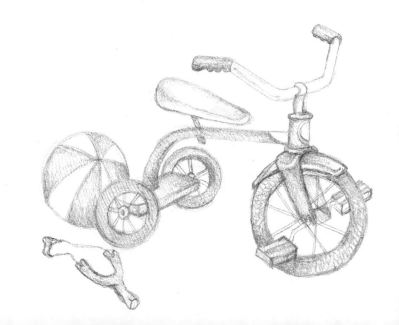

Children do not remain children forever, and parents, while retaining the title for life, become 'parents emeriti.'

Phyllis Theroux

The wolf also shall dwell with the lamb, and the leopard shall lie down with the kid; and the calf and the young lion and the fatling together, and a little child shall lead them.

Isaiah

All that I am or hope to be I owe to my mother.
Abraham Lincoln

A child's tears move the heavens themselves.
                                    Jewish proverb

New parents quickly learn that raising children is a kind of desperate improvisation.

Bill Cosby

A mother understands what a child does not say.
Jewish proverb

I think, at a child's birth, if a mother could ask a fairy godmother to endow it with the most useful gift, that gift would be curiosity.

Eleanor Roosevelt

In any other situation this would be called schizophrenia—maybe that's one reason mothers don't talk with childless friends about the work they do. It's wonderful work, but not 100 percent in the realm of the rational.

Liz Rosenberg

If the world will ever be redeemed, it will be through the virtues of children.

Jewish proverb

Having a child is surely the most beautifully irrational act that two people in love can commit.

Bill Cosby

What I pray for this year is not the remission of my sins, but the wit to remember them when they come back to me as my offspring's.

William Gibson

What tigress is there that does not purr over her young ones, and fawn upon them in tenderness.

St. Augustine

Though parents have a dozen children, each is the only one.
Jewish proverb

A baby is an inestimable blessing and a bother.
Mark Twain

Childhood is frequently a solemn business for those inside it.
George F. Will

Perhaps a better woman, after all,
With chubby children hanging on my neck
To keep me low and wise.
                    Elizabeth Barrett Browning

*Cosby's First Law of Intergenerational Perversity: no matter
what you tell your child to do, he will always do the opposite.*
Bill Cosby

For me, a line from my mother is more efficacious than all the homilies preached in Lent.

Henry Wadsworth Longfellow

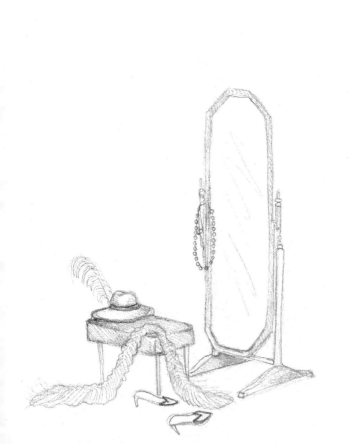

While our children are struggling to discover who they are, we parents are their first full-length mirrors. The power of our reflections is very strong indeed.

Phyllis Theroux

A child's simple sense is a kind of wisdom.
Jewish proverb

In some ways you go through motherhood in an under-siege mentality. You never admit how hard things are till they're safely behind you.

Liz Rosenberg

Stories heard at mother's knee are never wholly forgotten—a little spring that never quite dries up in our journey through scorching years.

Ruffini

All that I am my mother made me.
John Quincy Adams

Whosoever shall humble himself as this little child, the same is the greatest in the kingdom of heaven.

The Gospel of Matthew

We parents so often blow the business of raising kids, but not because we violate any philosophy of child raising. I doubt there can be a philosophy about something so difficult, something so downright mystical as raising kids.

Bill Cosby

Wherever children are learning, there dwells the Divine Presence.

Jewish proverb

One good mother is worth a hundred schoolmasters.
George Herbert

I marvel at their uniqueness, their thought processes, their deepening capacity to respond to life, to wake up glad to be alive, to roll with the punches that occasionally knock them down.

Phyllis Theroux

An ounce of mother is worth a pound of clergy.
Spanish proverb

For all intents and purposes, I might as well be a street mime, communicating to my children without words what I've spent the past twenty years being extremely vocal about: values, behavior, the Meaning of Life.

Phyllis Theroux

It is safer in a mother's lap than in a lord's bed.
Estonian proverb

There's something about babies that reminds us about how precious life is—not that we haven't known it all along. But they don't allow us to forget it for an instant.

Liz Rosenberg

I have always regretted I am not as wise as the day I was born.

Henry David Thoreau

I missed being an elevator boy by just that much, when my mother reached up and made me go back to school after laying out for two years.

Lyndon B. Johnson

When your kid is sick all perspective slides into the ocean.
Liz Rosenberg

You know the only people who are always sure about the proper way to raise children? Those who've never had any.
Bill Cosby